# The Calming Presence

A Book of Poetry

Georgette Dahl

Georgette Dahl
Copyright © GEORGETTE DAHL, 2024
All Rights Reserved. No part of this bookshall be reproduced, stored in a retrieval system, or transmitted by any means electronically, mechanically, photocopy, recording, or otherwise without written permission from Georgette Dahl.

Dahl, Georgette.
The Calming Presence / by Georgette Butler
**ISBN:** 9798343595550
Bahamian Poetry
Independently Published

Design & Layout
Cloudbar Designs L.L.C.
Orlando, Florida (407) 860-6774

info@cloudbardesigns.com, www.cloudbardesigns.com

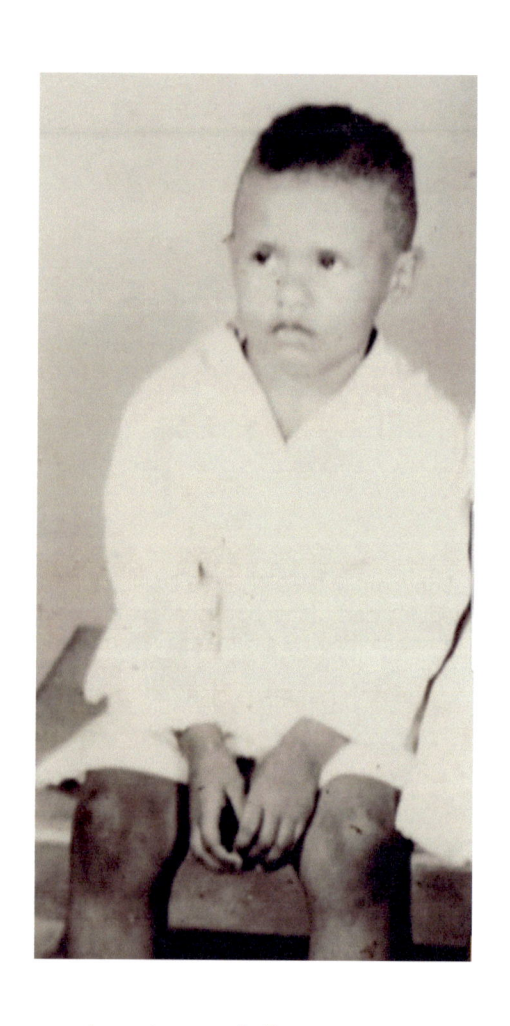

Weeds must be cleared for New Grass to grow.

# Dedication

To my brother
Anthony George Dahl
Mi querido hermano Anthony
(My dearest brother)

Abeja (Honey bee)

A play writer, an author of books on literature and History

Honoured his culture with the use of poetry

Historian and Educator who
Spoke seven languages.
Love to share his knowledge and uplift others not only by his presence but the kind words spoken.
I wish to continue his love for the Arts and his love of Poetry.

To you Tonkie Dahl

# CONTENTS

Introduction

The Calming Presence

The Author

Broken

Sailing

Our Existence

Words

Just Breathe

When I Choose me there is no you

A Tribute to Mr. Egerton Chang

"The Hummingbird"

Mi Querido hermano Anthony

Oh Captain! Great Captain

Quick Time

A Mother's Love

You Don't see me

Adornare

Another day above ground

Soigne'

Greetings My Beloved "Tony'

Padma

The Shadow

Baby I'm Beautiful

Crown and Glory

There's a Brown Girl in the Ring "Tra la lal la la la"

'Say my name, Say my name

**Freedom Is**

F - *faith*
R - *revived that*
E - *emanates*
E - *every time*
D - *doubt*
O - *occupies the*
M - *mind*

# Introduction

Poetry can bring to life passion, expression, and the imagination
Our thoughts can create space to live
To breathe
Yet like water it finds its own level
In the sea we find our calming presence
Water raging is the mind unsettled
And the movement itself is wordless and silent
The light of hope is sometimes dim
Our faith lay dormant within
Yet we embrace the darkness of night as our solitude
Often running ahead to catch the nameless shadow not understanding that it is our own reflection
We look at others, our world and adjust our lenses to see what is in the many villages in our globe
Forgetting and forsaking the naked eye's view of who we are
The tragedy of our living is that we are mistaken and often misunderstood!
You will not see me because you are too busy looking at you
We then resolve to JUST BREATHE

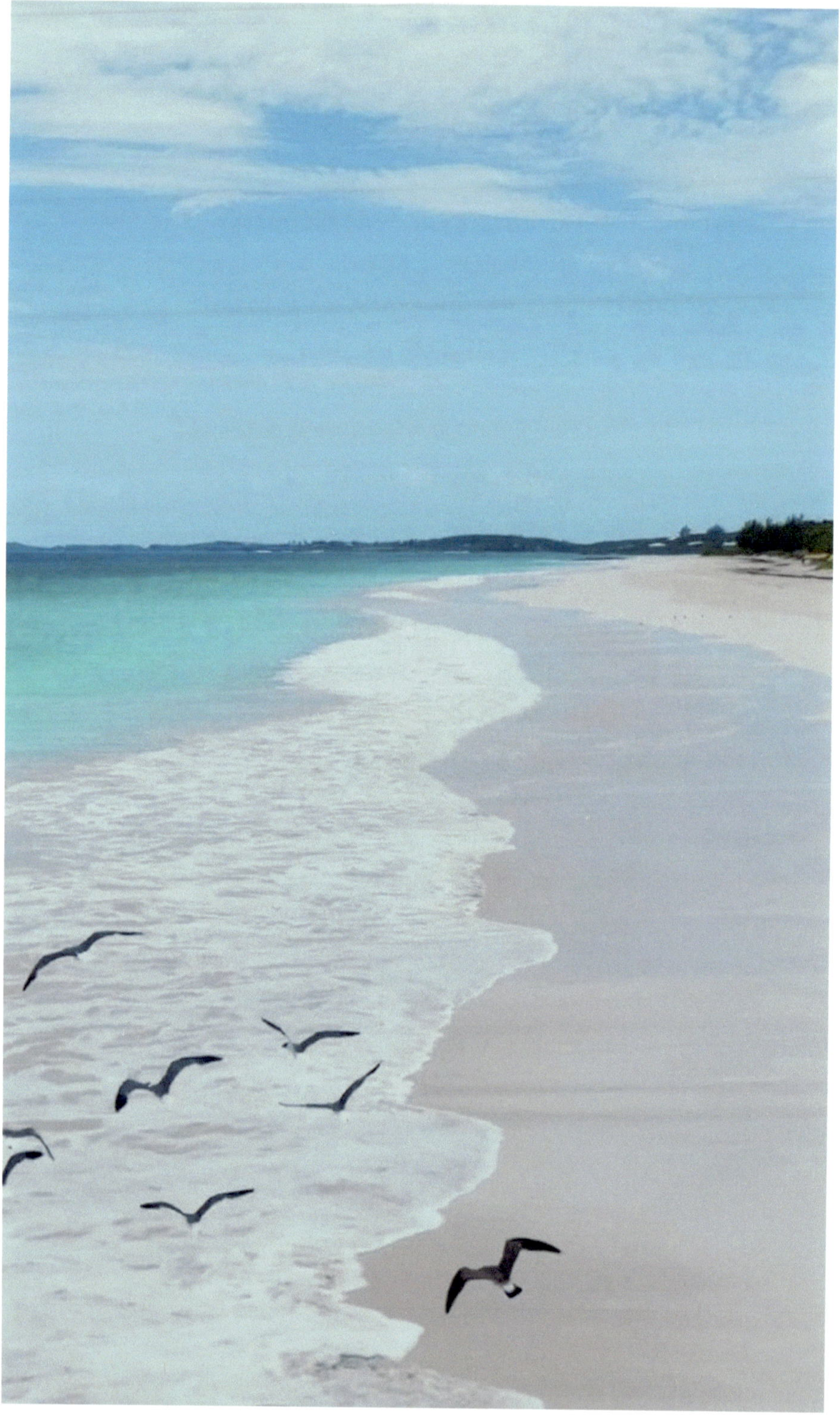

Self Love

Self-Worth

Freedom of Choice

Every Breath You Take

Chartered Path in Unchartered Waters

Restoration/Resilience

# The Calming Presence

The whisper of the sea waves echoes in my ear.
The purity of the unpolluted air tingles on my scalp and breezes through my hair
Without permission I can leave my soul at the shoreline, and it will not disappear.
Instead, the medicinal features in the saltwater will heal and repair.

The sea holds many of our secrets.
Allowing us to speak our thoughts out loud.
Without a reply and without another sound
No judgement on what is said,
No apologies to the living or to the dead
We speak what is on the mind even those words that are unsaid.

The sea has the calmness and gives peace of mind.
Said to cleanse the troubled soul time after time.
While it remains Mysterious it is free
No restrictions, No boundaries
It appears unending transforming its presence in shades of green and blue,
Majestic, soothing yet courageous and always appears brand new,
Represents freedom from the confinement of life,
While roaming aimlessly in the dark of night

Often, we are anchored in the quicksand of untruths,
Gasping for air only to make it through,
Remembering the bad feelings, we once knew
Expecting our bodies to remain afloat,
Without a canoe or a boat

With no directions given
Without a Captain or a first mate
We are vulnerable surrendering our thoughts and allowing the wind to navigate,
Just as the winds blow creating unsettled life,
The gushing waves beat against the firmness of a strong heart,
It can't withstand the strength, it falls apart,
Yet the smell of salt is in the air and the taste upon lips,
Believing that there is a point of no return from this lonely trip,
Abandoned without any land in sight,
Lost paddles it's dark and there is no light.

Life represents nothing more than what one believes,
Peace in spirit can be achieved,
Relieve the mind of the uncontrolled things to the calmness of the seas,
Allow it to claim those vicarious thoughts and toss them to the gentle breeze,
The Calming presence is in you and in me
I find The Calming presence as I gaze upon the Sea!!

# Purpose

When the authenticity of who we are emerges
and
we respect ourselves,
and our love embraces our inner and outer boundaries of self,
the once voiceless soloist is granted permission to sing its truth
without whispering,
the audible sounds permeate the inner soul,
abolishing the outer boundaries that we have designed for
ourselves,
thus, creating newness of purpose within our lives

**Photography Paola Wells**

15 | *The Calming Presence*

# The Author

You are the Author of the book called life
Start with a pen and never an erasable pencil
Accept that some parts of your life, you can never erase
or re-sharpen the pencil so that they appear pretty and clean
Embrace those seemingly unforgiving moments
Learn from them and forgive yourself
No one charters your course in life or pens your journey
Love you first with all the inerasable parts of you
Remember they too have value and truth
Tell yourself that defeat is not a word for me
The word known to me is fait accompli
You can decide whether to be happy, sad, mean or simply nice
As you are the author, publisher and editor of your life

# Broken

Broken like shattered glass
Constantly repeating the past
Attempting to mend with crazy glue
Pieces are not fitting together as if brand new
I pour water into my glass only to find the smallest crack
There is once again a set back
Tried time after time to repair
Longing for attention that was just not there
Trying to restore my belief and faith
Rapidly losing hope
Drowning in sorrow everyday
Dependent on the peace from a New Day
Hoping for a life of complete restoration
Longing for respect, love and adoration
No remorse but continuous lies
Told they're not real but in the mind
Called delusional to cover up the crime
Trusted and destroyed by deceit
Needed affirmation to be whole and complete
Not understanding it was lack of confidence in me
That succumbed to the lies and made me weak
On the mend with eyes wide open
Never to be destroyed or to be broken

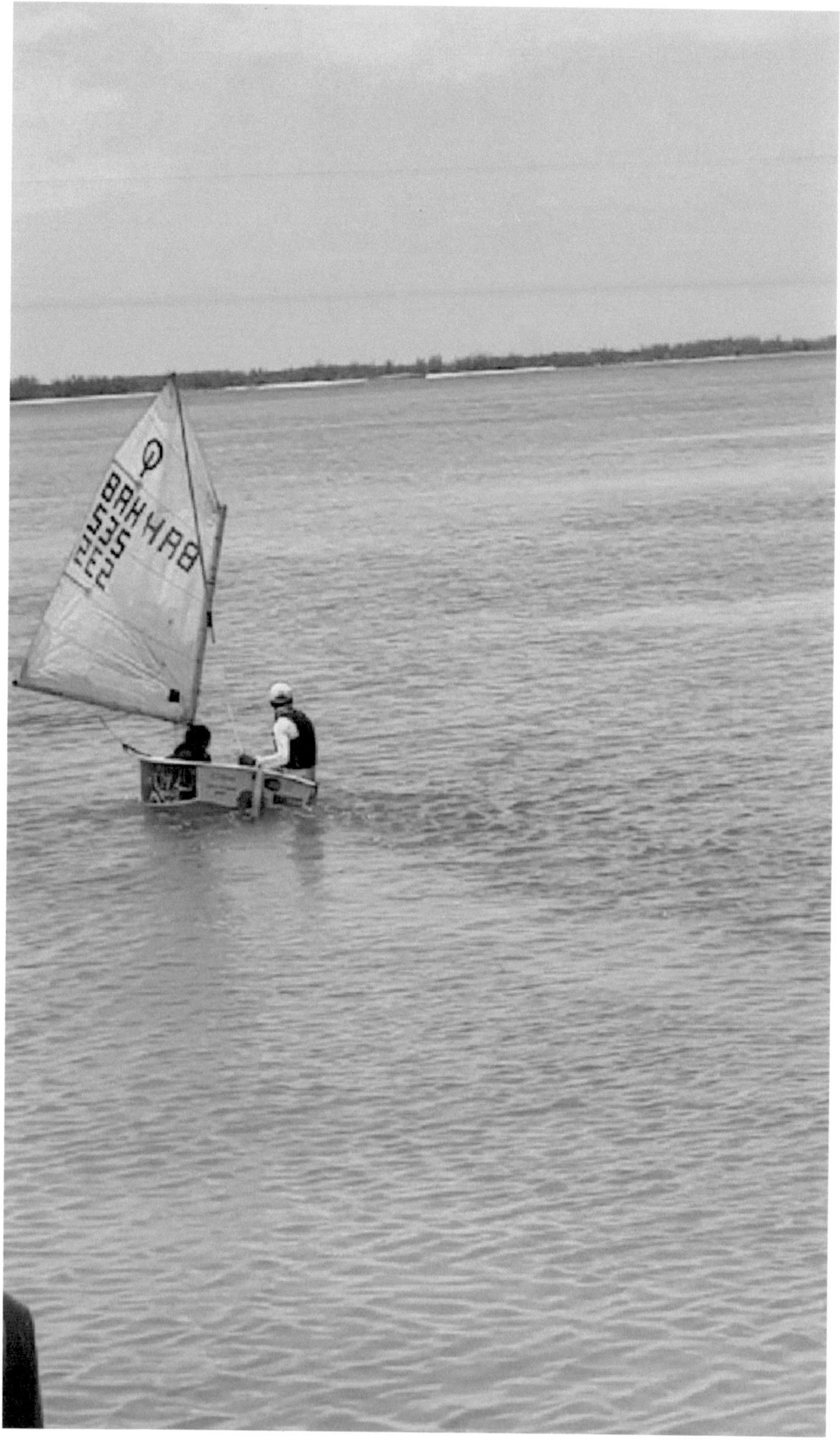

# Sailing

The Sea represents freedom for many
No boundaries, no restriction
It appears unending transforming in hues of blue
allowing the minds soberness of what is true
Can move with the poise and composure of a trained dancer
Yet can switch to the careless movement of a raging bull who can be
a prancer
It maintains an unspoiled serene beauty as natures gift
Never hesitating to take lives as the raging waves shift
Can be a bully and unkind
Can be a gentle soul at times
Fear not for the Sea holds many treasures
For you to find

# SELF

Our words mirror our thoughts
Often a reflexion of
Self
Experience
Gratitude and grace
We constantly seek attention and admiration
Negating self-worth
Yet anticipating appreciation
There are many battles and storms we will be required to fight
Self-love is your only weapon in times of war
It is the resilient and reliable armour
That is often ignored

# Words

It is said that "Silence is Golden"
Words speaks volumes even the ones unspoken
Feeding the spirit when damaged and broken
Words can bring peace within
In times when there is no hope, and the world is dim
And the war on disease we may never win
In times of turmoil, I am lost for words
My voice has disappeared without a trace, I can't be heard
I send the search party with a flashlight to find my inner thoughts
For the words have disappeared and won't come forth
Proverbs 15:4 says, "Gentle words bring life and health".
The war and disease around me make all words felt
I use them to uplift with the right tone and sound
hoping that a cure would soon be found
Using words that are encouraging and motivating,
Transforming our emotions to positive thoughts while communicating
Our words can inspire others in need
even when they don't believe
Words are the foundation for our conversations
used incorrectly could destroy an entire nation
Our words say who we are
Positive vibrations of our words can be felt from a far
Remembering how great they made you feel
Those beautiful words with the power to heal
when our doubts and hopes we fight to ignore
Words have the power to reassure

Words matter to me and to you
In a world where uncertainty is true
Encouraging words can add value too

## "JUST BREATHE"

## Pain/Shame

When I have masked and compressed my pain and shame
I'm left with the phenolic acids, the nutrient, and the sharpness of the rind.
Which awakes my body and soul as I embrace my power of choice, of truthfulness and forgiveness of self

# JUST BREATHE

When guilt and shame has stripped us naked as the day we were born
No clothes to cover or to put on,
When all those we characterized as friends that we depended on have turned their backs and are now gone,
There is only a mirror exposing oneself in its truest form,
Yet we hold our gaze adjusting our posture upright with chin raised,
Embracing our flaws
Banishing the thoughts of unworthiness
While owning our truth more and more
Acknowledging that the voices from the crowd has silenced our once loud voice and we are now speechless,
And the vulnerability we feel is looked at as a sign of weakness,
Finding ourselves in a fetal position and then on all fours crawling like a baby on the floor
No clapping, no applause
No longer favoured but ignored,
What happened to the life we had before we invited shame?
And we decided we would play the victim in the blame game?
Blinded and not seeing ourselves as the picture in the broken frame,
Recognizing that all material manner that once defined us has disappeared,
We are now defined by how we respond, and we hold our tongue in fear,
If we choose to dwell in the past
We enter the future with baggage and wearing a shameful mask,
we then become someone else's forgotten history,
Forbidding our Vulnerability to seek empathy,
Shame cannot survive speakability,
Give self-worth a moment please,
Take a deep breath and
JUST BREATHE

# Selfish or Self Less

We continue to wait and hope for others to change,
Often suffering through the metamorphosis
Only to find it was not them but ourselves (us)
Our disempowered and dysfunctional selves needed,
the transformation, the affirmation called courage to self-love.

# When I Choose Me There is No YOU

We sometimes struggle within
Our troubled unsettled soul
Waiting and anticipating love, that never unfolds
Some persons don't possess the ability to reciprocate.
They're not able to communicate
The inability to show kindness.
To have emotions
To partner, to love, to feel.
Is never true and often unreal.
Yet we run to rescue their hurt, their pain.
Jeopardising and masking our own sorrow and never complain
Often defeated by the lack of care or thought shown
Yet we make excuses for lack of values which to us is unknown
When we realize that our people projects are our own emptiness
And the continued giving of oneself can lead to jealousy and contempt
Reflection of self should not be said to be selfless or selfish
It's our way of choosing me first
In the battle to our right to life
The realization that I matter too
Is convincing myself and my psyche that it is true
When I know that I choose me
And there is no more you to please
I have run the race to the finish line with ease
My heart rest as there is no defeat but only peace
This is my truth, and I do believe
by choosing me there is no YOU

# THESE ARE YOUR STORIES

## WARRIORS

## VISIONARIES

## HEROS

## CHAMPIONS

## CAPTAINS

## COURAGEOUS

## LIFE CONQUERORS

# A Tribute to Mr. Egerton Chang

### "The Hummingbird"

The man I met was a "Statesman" whose qualities were unique
A principled person possessing the moral compass that made him complete
No ordinary man but entrancing in speech
Had an iridescent glow about his face
Spoke with knowledge and unending grace
His spirit encapsulated life's enjoyment
While his body did not succumb to life's confinement

He was resilient, smart and quick
A generous man who didn't nit-pick

He had conquered life's challenges in many ways
Respected by those who would have met him for the first time, even today

As the heavenly doors open, we pray
For the safe journey of our beloved "Hummingbird"
Egerton Chang who has passed away.

Your family in the Bahamas

# Our Existence

We choose to live in the past
Even when images are blurred, and memories lost
We rewind the clocks with anticipation that time will remain at a standstill
Opening the sutures that once sealed our wounds and guarded our past
Preserving our thoughts only to torment our minds and disrupt our inner peace
In the chaos and untruth of life where we destroy our own happiness
Time gives us the legitimacy to know we exist
As we turn our hourglasses upside down to measure
It is time that releases our energy and gives us power that proves our existence does matter

# Mi querido hermano Anthony
### (My dearest brother)
### Abeja (Honey bee)

A Gentle soul was he
Gave persons limits and set boundaries
His knowledge of books gave him joy and peace.
He was able to regurgitate what he read when he spoke
His vocal range was that of a Tenor and the falsetto's was a delight to the ear.
Could play songs on the piano simply by air
He could say the Anglican mass in Latin it's true
Poor pronunciation of words would make him blue
Spoke languages of many kinds
Taught Spanish and Portuguese at Spelman for 25 years!
"that's a long time"
Was a play write an author of books on literature and History
Traced culture with the use of poetry
Always punctual, clean, meticulous, and neat
When entering his house, he required shoe removal from your feet

Gave me my name like his he would say
Put up a protective gate at home so that I would not run away
Taught me German on the way to school
Made me believe when I spoke, I was cool
I rolled my tongue just as I was told
And pronounced my words properly so I would not be scolded

One could never win an argument with him
As his rebuttals made you give in
Was the family Guava Duff man
Until Asia took over the kitchen, this was not the plan
If he got upset, he would cut his eyes, suck his teeth, giggle then smile
One would say Wow! He was only upset for a short while
Loved Classical music and the opera for sure
Never forgetting his roots in negro folklore
Was gentle, prolific, caring yet stern
passionate about his students and their ability to learn
Spent his last days picking up Chris in the afternoon
The drive was long, and he could pretend he was teaching and back in school
Tony is moving his head and singing his favourite song
"I can see clearly now the rain is gone"
And he would say
I have walked the last mile of the way
Release me please
Release me into the sea
The nomad is at peace
And now set me free

# Oh Captain! Great Captain!

This ship set sail on May 7th, 2002
The captain of whom we speak, It's you
Your seven-pound body was compact and unique
Your eyes, Your hands and even Your feet
Were perfectly designed to say the least
We worried when you did not speak
But when you did your sentences were nothing short of complete
A Stateman who is wise beyond his years
Possessing Sovereign qualities, Values and the Morals only you could bear
An Orator with knowledge of history that many will want to hear
A natural born leader with little fear
Created a platform on a firm foundation that's all you
Never waving in your undeniable philosophy or your truth
A Visionary in many ways
You rise to face a challenge on any given day
You're not consumed by your own ascendancy
Firm in your own beliefs, unconcerned about others sense of superiority
As you set forth to sail on this journey called life
May you hoist your sail high while bringing reason to a world full of strife
You're the captain who puts others first so they may not fall
Will try your best to protect us all
Oh Captain! Great Captain
J. Christopher Butler

Love: Mom

33 | *The Calming Presence*

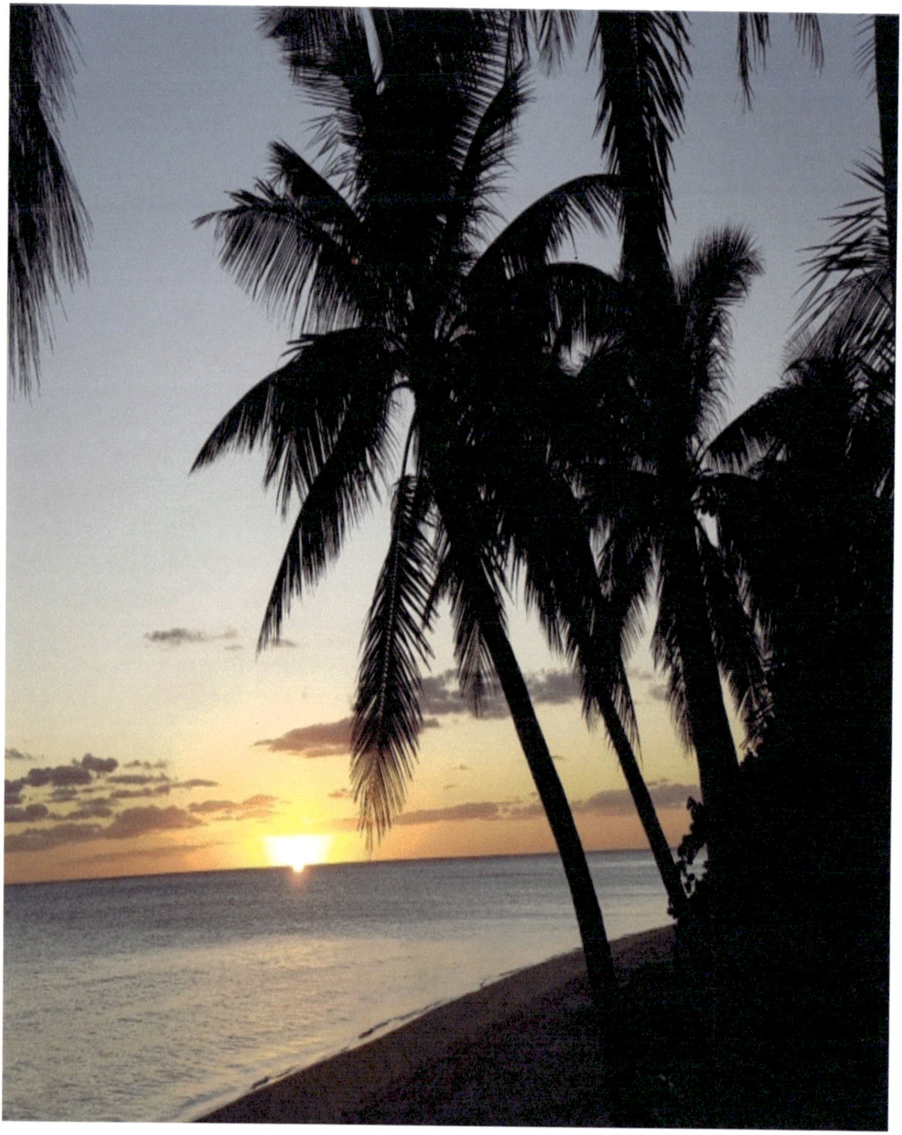

# Quick Time

I wake up in a hurry
Knowing everything is time
I say my prayers quickly
So at least that's done on time
I wonder where my life is going, no break that I call mine
The work is there to do, and one must comply with the deadline
My Mother prayed for her children
For health, strength and peace of mind
She asked that her home going would be the best anyone would see in their life time
She said this life; this breath is not your own
Give it to Jesus who sits upon the Throne
My soul wonders into space
My body continues to work quickly at a fast pace
Will I have time to stand before the Throne?
To confess my sins that I dare not own
Will he know the quick prayer person with no time of her own?
Maybe not! as her name remains unknown

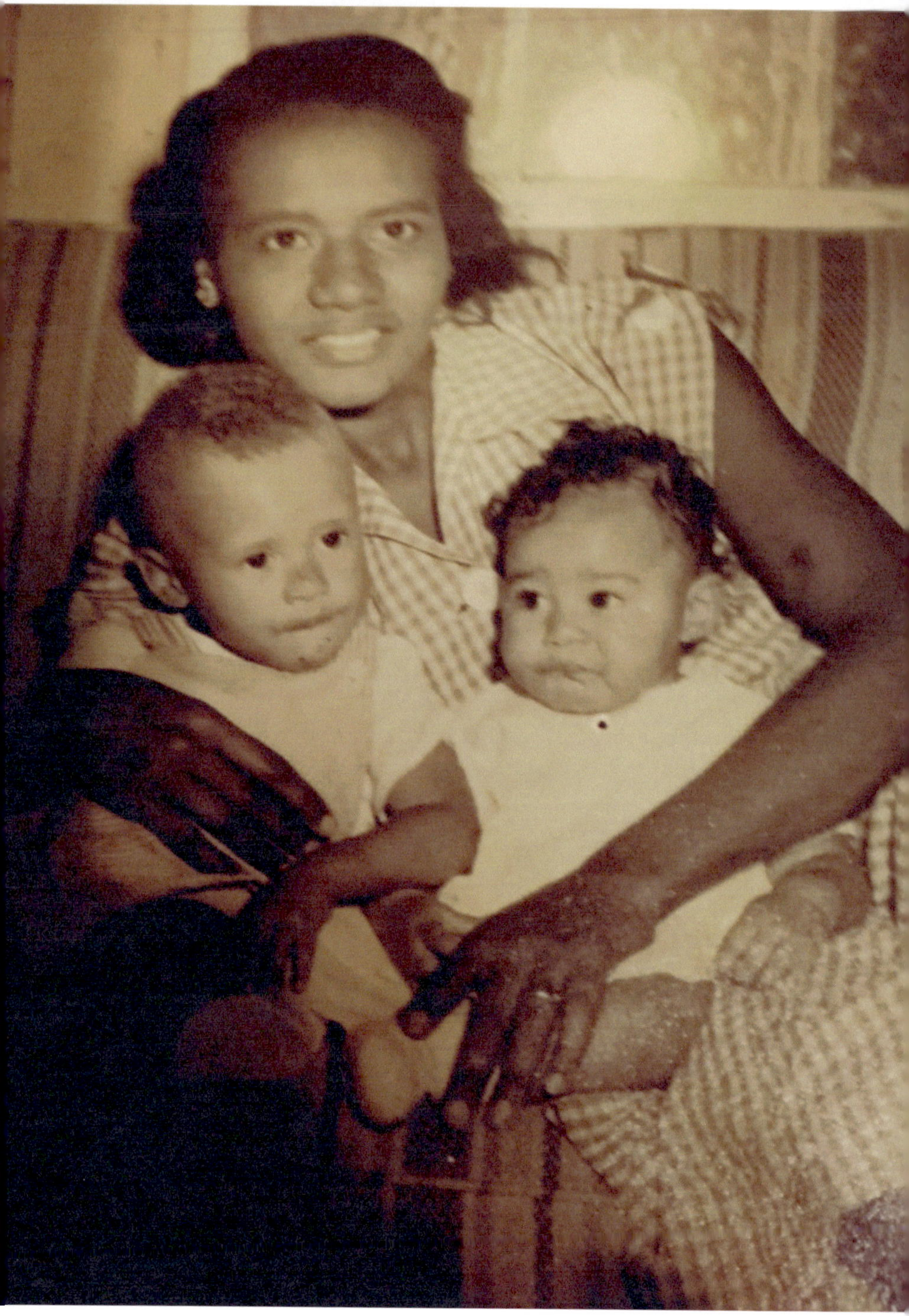

# A Mother's Love

A Mother's love is special
Some say divine
It has no limits, it sets no time
It is selfless in expression, it's warm, It's kind

She carries her children's worries, their pain
And ask for nothing in return, this I can't explain!
She cries for her children when they have no tears left that they can find
And protects them with unending Pride

Never ask for gifts or rewards for her love
She is content with the love from God above
Her love is unconditional, and some say it's blind
It matters not as she gives it at the right time

She would count my fingers and my toes
And then she would kiss my nose
Her warm embrace was unopposed
I would melt in her arms while my eyes remained closed
Absorbing the love from a mother that only a child knows.

# YOU DON'T SEE ME

When you look at the exterior
It is only a mirror image of self
The reflection of composure
Forgotten soul waring has no exposure
Wrapped up neatly inside a carved-out space
Can't be unlocked can't even escape
You see my eyes, my nose, my lips
What about my soul, my heart?
That beats and sometimes skips

You Don't see me

You only see those big brown beautiful eyes
But you can't see what I hide inside
The blood that runs through my veins
Is filled with love and often pain

You Don't see me

The Mask:
Asia Butler grade 8

The soul reaching for peace, reaching for life
It's a struggle it's a fight
The appearance is glowing
The spirit is not free, it's not flowing

You Don't see me

I pretend it's alright
I smile for the camera and blink at the flashlight
Sometimes I cry, I lie
Reviving my faint heartbeat before the sound dies
Sometimes I'm true
Pretending not to be blue

You Don't see me
because you're too busy looking at you

**Photography Gerad Smith**

*40 | The Calming Presence*

*You don't see me because you're too busy looking at you!*

**Ivana and Her Father**

# ADORNARE

("PATER" Father)
Like the beautiful, detailed woodwork on the stern of a ship
He is the ship's Hull and comes fully equipped
Can withstand any load including that of a thousand bricks
Exercising caution to prevent anything seemingly tragic
Manoeuvring through the world untold
Emulating the actions and values of the men of old
He is the Admiral who leads the family while maintaining control

He may never appear to sink or drown
Except to succumb to his children's sad faces or their frown
He has the Strength of a warrior ship if he needs to fight
A protector for his family a protector of their life
Anchored firm unwavering in what he believes
With the strength of Iron and sometimes steel
Yet possessing the powerful compassion to bend and to feel

Solid as the rock of Gibraltar never to be questioned or moved
Only for his children's love which he approves
Firm on principles of what is right
With Fidelity and Truth, he stands upright
Like the sail of a ship, he is hoisted high with pride.
To direct, cultivate and to guide
The "Pater" (Father) of whom we see
Possesses the fortitude, Dexterity, and agility.
Anchored firm in strength, love, and Integrity

# Another Day Above Ground

I look upon my face of old
Each line has a story untold
The laugh lines are indeed my happy times
The crow's feet they're unique
They tell my stories of when I squinted in disbelief
My lips that I once said pucker up
They are thin and may have dropped
My cheeks were once full and rosy they said
Now sunken in but I'm not dead
My teeth are pearly white
Because of the dentures I take out at night
I wear glasses to read the words on the wall
It's not my fault they made the prints so small
I forget sometimes
It's because I have a lot on my mind
I call each child's name aloud
Until the right one is found
My waist was small and neat
With the use of a girdle to make it smooth and complete
Now with the use of elastic in the waist
It helps to accommodate the expanded space
My heart would beat rapidly in the past
I am grateful to have a beat that lasts
I often have pain
But no use to complain
I know I am not the same
But I haven't forgotten my maiden name.
And although I may need a walking stick
It's for me to decide which one I'll pick
I am at an age where what I say is right
and you're not allowed to launch a fight
I hear when I want to hear you speak
Otherwise, I pretend the hearing aid needs to be tweaked.

I am who I was meant to be
No regrets of the life given to me
Created great individuals whom I called my own
They have left me as they are all grown
No longer children of mine
Created their own families to last their lifetime
As my eyes opened in the early morn
I thank God for affording me another day added to the day I was born
I have no reason to fret or frown
As it's another day above ground

# Another Day Above Ground

**Mrs. Williams 95 years old**

To Succeed is when Your

S – Strength and Support is
U – Unequivocal to the
C – Compassion that meets
C – Commitment and the
E – Empowered self
E – Embraces
D – Determination

# Soigné

Photography Paola Wells

48 | The Calming Presence

# Soigné

Like Sandro Botticelli's painting "THE BIRTH OF VENUS"
Emerges the Island girl with a purpose
Crafted in the eyes of Greek goddess Aphrodite
Charming, quick and can appear feisty
A unique lady is she
Possessing peace, kindness, and simplicity
Her smile is infectious to all she meets
Even animals and strangers on the streets
She's the fairy who throws pixie dust upon your face and upon your feet
Giving out a heart full of love as she greets
Takes on a challenge and willing to work
Not to be disturbed by others for fear of fireworks
Constantly seeking knowledge and is analytical
Innovative and logical
Exercises self-control
While adhering to proper protocol
Sophisticated, elegant, poised and refined
A lady with a gentle heart that will last a lifetime
A millionaires' confidence in her walk and in her style
Self-motivated and does not need affirmation or approval.
A survivor who is content and sometimes immovable
Seeking growth and improvement yet humble when she smiles
Empowering others along the way
While displaying class, manners in her presence day after day
She has a mystery in her glow
Will stare you in the face when frustrated so you know how far to go
She competes only with herself and is dignified
Never afraid to say what's on her mind
A lady with substance and is refined
with a grateful heart
Soigné! très Soigné a work of Art

# Greetings My Beloved "Tony"

My Beloved, my dear
I am well and there is no need to fear.
I ask that you do not shed tears.
For we have loved each other more than thirty plus years.

I am in my father's house.
I promise I did not pick a fight,
I am as quiet as a mouse,
His arms were wide open as I walked through the heavenly gate,
He smiled and hugged me saying "Michelle you're not late",

Our memories we have both memorised,
No pretence and no disguise
My heavy breathing you loved to hear,
Knowing I was alive and oh so near,
I miss you, as you miss me too,
The silent room is the peace I give to you,
Know that my heart is full of love for you,
Cherish the moments with no regrets but, only what's true,
I hear our song playing right now,
I am watching the Angels as they take a bow,
"MICHELLE MY BELL"
You're smiling I can tell,
My beautiful fragrance you recognize,
And hold your breath; Aww!! as you inhale my heavenly smell,

I wish you happiness and good health above all,
My departure was to make you strong, and I don't expect you to fall,
Know that the emptiness you feel inside,
Is temporary because I'm always by your side,
Remember I was on loan to you my love,
All debts paid by God above,

I will not see you in the morning or at noon,
Hope to see you sometime soon,
You're never alone,
Michelle is now at home,
With all my love
"MICHELLE"

**Tony and Michelle**

## Padma

My heart took flight,
In the gentle breeze in the dark of night
Bellicus was defeated
Like the words to a favourite song simply deleted
The unseen bruises generated great pain,
Yet no one to cast blame,
Loss of faith and hope made me wish many would forget my name.
My compass had to be reset,
As the pendulum swings back and forth time does not honour regret
Submerged in the dark of night,
To the disappearing sunlight
The soul anchored in muddy waters of life,
Yet emerges in the morning sparkling clean and bright,
Uncontaminated freed from the depths of pain
Overcoming life's conflict, judgement and shame
The strength of the soul conquered adversity
While trusting itself to unfold naturally
Reaching the surface of spiritual awakening
Imbibe thoughts of divine goodness
The mind discerns the truth finding the equilibrium of dignity, abundance and auspiciousness.
Like Lakshmi the goddess of wealth who grants success in all endeavours
Yahweh is the beautiful rebirth that keeps us centred.

When your values are not aligned
And your worthiness suppressed.
The imposter is vindicated.
While taking up temporary Residence
in your space

Love

L - Life's

O - Oxygen

V - Vulnerability

E - Empathy

COLOURLESS

FLAWLESS

PRICELESS

BOUNDLESS

BODACIOUS

BEAUIFUL AND PROUD

# "The Shadow"

*Photographer: Niko Cloud*

# Light Truth

We often operate in the unconsciousness of darkness.
Constantly repeating to ourselves past events thus, giving credit to our false truth
We do this consistently until we and others believe it.
We lack the courage to face the light, for fear of judgement.
Therefore, we embrace our inertia, our sameness that we characterise as whole.
While uplifting and expanding our broken ego's
Without being brave enough to submit our truth to the brightness of the light

# The Shadow

My shadow appears before me in daylight.
It's a solider at attention.
Often enlarged but disappears at night.
It stands afar like a silhouette of self.
The linear lines tell me it's not anyone else.
I try to hide in the unconsciousness of the night.
Only to find the shadow reappears in the sunlight.
Am I the victim of the choice's others have made?
Understanding that choices are like scars they seldom fade.
I've honoured others' mistakes by adopting them as my own,
Suffering through the criticism and hiding when someone else threw the first stone.
Yet I'm expected to remain anonymous and unknown,
As you steal my identity and leave me standing all alone
Like a chameleon I blend into the color of the wall
While my shadow still stands tall
I gaze in the pool of water, not seeing my reflection but that of another.
The little boy with tears in his eyes, carrying the troubles of the world inside.
Through time I have healed and blossomed
I am the flower in the garden unique.
My petals communicate in a wordless language understood by all.
While my fragrance permeates in winter, summer, spring, and fall.
Prince self-adorned yet admired by all.
The shadow that was once lost in the dark of night.
By giving my unconscious darkness, the light
Emerging from life's struggles, hardship, and fight
To bloom in the morning light
Acknowledging my worth and now my right to life I am the shadow that stands tall when there is no Sunlight.

# Baby I'm Beautiful

Ebony coloured pulchritudinous woman full of substance and charm
Alluring and hypnotic leaving one spellbound
Perfect in symmetry from head to toe
Only Fibonacci numbers could complete the Golden ratio
The body designed with aesthetic integrity
Sculptured in detail with Gods divinity,
truly unique and one of a kind
Put on earth to be cherished by mankind

As graceful as a Swan with poise, elegance, and great vision
Can fly with the burden of life's weight in the worst condition
Likened to beauty of the Hindu goddess Parvati and Helen of Troy
Her presence demands an encore as it brings eminent joy

Known to stop traffic on a highway in the south
Eyes widening along with the mouth
The curvaceous hips
The heart shaped voluptuous lips
exquisite kinky hair adorned with ribbon and tucked in with clips
captivates the heart as the beat skips

Drivers in passing cars slow down to rubberneck
mesmerized as they perform a closer check
YES!! you saw right
Hips and thighs big yet tight
Breast uplifted infinite

Almond shaped eyes with a dark hue
Penetrates the heart that's pure and true
Naked and uninhibited as the day I was born
The Greeks called it a perfection of the Gods, no covering, no shoal
Just a Woman who is completely whole
We call it the uniform of the Soul
That cares and nurtures and gets better in years of old
Western world through Christianity labelled it a sin and a shame
Forgetting Adam and Eve was the original name

We judge by complexion
While lusting at perfection

We learn love, fear and hate
Develop religious beliefs and call it our faith
Yet we can never escape
Our destiny or our fate

It's indisputable
Baby I'm Beautiful

# "Baby I'm Beautiful"

Painting by Malcolm Rea

# Silence

My silence is not because I don't acknowledge you
It is because I have learnt that my response is invaluable
And I choose to be judicious and prudent

# Crown And Glory

Nappy hair, kinky hair, straight hair, good hair
Whether our complexion was dark, light or fair
Our identifier, our strength
Feared by others as powerful in length
Cut like Samson to be weakened
Shaved by masters' and beaten
The unspeakable crime we faced
Ridding slaves of their identity and their race
To gain control and dependency
Stripping one of status and ethnicity

Good hair!! Black women would ask of God when they pray
It was the softer wavy locks when combed and needed little product or spray
Eurocentric some may say
Genes mixed in the unconventional way
Considered pretty and master could demand more pay
Tight spiral curls, Nappy, Woolly, Kinky hair was despised
Yet our braided styles were stolen by many cultures, no surprise
Fishtail, cornrow, French braids, box braids, rope braids to name a few
The Afro as a symbol of rebellion, pride and empowerment was adopted too
Even the rooted tree like long "Natty" locks matted that grew
Was admired and worn by races who thought Kinky was taboo
Our hair represents heritage, strength, culture, identity, and power,
Said to be the pathway to the Soul often adorned with feathers, beads, or flowers,
Dismissed, undermined and misunderstood due to its seemingly coarse texture,
Madam C J Walker hair care helped eliminate negative gestures
It is Spiritual, mystic often defines our Femininity
Not to mention our status in society
It's emotional, sensational with its own History
Respecting age, marital status, religion, and fertility

Due to Its close location to the skies the hair is not only seen as spiritual
It acts as an antenna and transmittable
Transmitting and receiving energies
Channelling the energy received from the sun forward, to our control panel the brain
That we use to meditate and often relieve pain

Natural, Kinky, Nappy hair said not to be the best
Not even Rapunzel is as proud and dignified when put to test
A crowning glory is the Nappy beautiful Tress

"The Afro"

Artist Lamont Missick

"Brown Girl in da Ring"

# There's a Brown Girl in The Ring
## TRA LA LA LA LA

Light skinned Caramel coloured girl on the scene
The attention grabber but never a part of the team
Straight hair down her back
Walked like a model as a matter of fact
She knows she is the preferred girl from the whistles of the boys when she "pass"
And even the men in cars who took their feet off the "gas"
Eyes popping as she swayed her more than generous hips
Unspoken words escape the lips

Playing into the dangerous views of this homogenous society
While adapting to prejudice of the 'brown paper bag theory"
Subjected to the reality of the colour hierarchy
Was the Brown girl in the ring

Mama black like midnight
Daddy like snow white
Brown girl could never look right
Brown girl in the ring
Privileged many would sing
Not feeling the sting
That a hostile society brings

High yellow, You're mellow
Red bone perfect tone
Light bright makes it alright
Brownin, don't need tannin
Half- caste gets no pass
Mangra skin, you win
Is this skin colour a curse and a sin?
Brown girl could never fit in

That was the Brown girl out the ring

# Brown Girl

Marcus Garvey's theory was that light skin mulatto blacks were inferior
Holding the darker skin as the standard of blackness that was superior
In a world where one lick of the tar brush says.
"you're Black,
Step back!"

Under the umbrella of the tinted hue
Whether black, brown, light, or mulatto you are discriminated against too
Discrimination not limited to the global view on Eurocentric beauty but,
hate within the same race
seen face to face

*Was the Brown girl out the ring*

Held down as fingernails dug into the face
Leaving scars that can be traced
Blackened eyes
to ensure Brown girl no longer a cutie pie
Hair pulled and deliberately chopped
Screaming until it stopped
A hot Iron heated on the stove for a day
to be planted upon the beautiful face
Not to be altered by God's grace
Please spare me I pray
The hand provided a barrier from the iron touching that forbidden space
As she was to be taught a lesson on beauty within her own race

*Brown girl out the ring*

Brown on brown hate was for all to see
Hair length and texture was the focus as she shouted at me.
"WAS YOUR FATHER WHITE!"
Were the words that spoke insecurity
With a grin and a smirk towards the reply
"My hair is softer than yours" was the loud cry
If your Butt was smaller you might pass for white
The struggle is real and so is the fight
Beauty is not within, it's by sight

He said, "You're my soul mate and beautiful too!"
Until the day I die I will love you
The ring bought for you, I will give to another
As she is not as beautiful said this black brother
I will marry her and give her a chance
Because the way you look you will always find romance

Brown girl without the ring

You're not black enough to be a part of the equality struggle or fight
You were still a slave, but in the house Light bright
Subjected to the same damming plight
Raped first both in the day and at night
But not considered dark enough in the fight for justice and what is right
Rejected by the lily white
Outcast as dingy yellow and, that made it alright

Brown girl out the ring
Tra la la la la

# Brown Girl

We are in a state of cognitive dissonance
Accepting that we are victimless
Where society is unapologetic
We capitulate while digressing
Enslaving ourselves in the war on skin colour
While succumbing to society's aesthetics
There's a Brown girl in the ring
Tra la la la la
In this unaccepting world, is she to seek Asylum?
Or dance to the beat of her own drum
And she looks like a sugar and a Plum Plum plum
Tra la la la la

Artist Lamont Missick

"Brown Girl out da Ring"

# Say My Name!! Say My Name!!!

What's your name? Puddin and Tane
What's your number,
Cucumber
On a scale of one to ten with one being white and ten being Black
I am number eleven.
Which meant I may be too dark to enter the gates of heaven?
I have been called many names but never Puddin and Tane
As for my number it was not Cucumber.
Perhaps infinity squared if there is such a number,
Growing up my Christian name was never said,
Other names I was called instead,
My names were Blackie, Darkie, Midnight, purple and sometimes darkest Blue,
Monkey, Black like Sparrow, Tar Baby too

I was only a young child a "baby".
When bleach was put in the water to bathe me
Made sure no water got in my eyes so that I could still see,
Said it was to make my skin soft,
No! It was to take the black off,
Fair and white was introduced to my life.
It was to make me pretty and bright,
Instead, I got sores and peeling and was burnt from the bleaching chemicals used to make me white.
The cliché no pain no gain
Cost of beauty and possible fame
Perhaps that should have been added to my name.

Words were written on the back of my shirt.
It was said to be my name to identify me in the childhood game.
Unbeknown, it read blackie Sambo,
Because of my colour I was said to be Bobo the Dumbo
This could not be.
Why would they hurt me?

They were my friends and family.

Even the little brown girl with crooked teeth
Stained dress and dirty feet
Discriminated against me
I was dirty.
She was sweet,
Even when not clean and neat

My hair was always neatly combed and straighten with a sheen,
Elastic bands and ribbons
Not white but green
Matching socks and Clark shoes polished with Vaseline,
Polka Dot dress
Powdered up to my neck,
My teeth were pearly white when checked,
My face scrubbed until my skin glistened while glean,
Yet still said to be dirty and unclean

My darkness embarrassed my own race.
The names they called me was directly to my face.
My sanctuary my home
Brought hurt untold.
As the different shades of black would unfold
Being the darkest in the family
My name was blackie.
Should I make an excuse and blame it on the ignorance of youth,
Or did they have a sober tongue like a drunkard and spoke the truth.

April was my best friend back in the day,
Hop scotched and jumped rope we played,
As she ran in her house the screen door slammed
Out of breath as I reached to push the door with my hand,
Ms. Justine pushed back and locked the screen,
The switch went across April's legs, and she screamed,
Heard Ms. say,
You better stay away!
"Why this poor Black ting following you today".

# Say My Name

It was not until someone darker sat by my side,
I refused to identify.
Was I the victim of this hurtful crime?
As I looked at her, I saw a reflection in the mirror that was all mine.
I discriminated against her darker hue,
Inflicting the only pain, I knew
Hurt and embarrassed as I carried the shame,
The words used by others for me I called her those names,
Grace Jones was the one to be admired,
Stood bold and alone and embraced her tone,
In an industry that was quick to throw stones
Mahalia Jackson, Jessye Norman and Nina Simone
Sang great songs and crossed the lenses of colour line.
"Four women", "Young gifted and Black" were sung at the precise time.
The music was divine,
At a time when black gifts were stolen and undermined.

**Artist Lamont Missick**

73 | *The Calming Presence*

# Say My Name

You look good for a black girl came out of the mouth,
A compliment of sorts, so, I thought,
If I lick your big juicy charcoal lips
Would it taste like chocolate chips?
Lick your pale pink lips,
does it taste like cotton candy that sticks?
Sad, a badly written script
When trying to get a kiss

Imprisoned in skin no doubt.
The bars on this cell have yet to be chiselled out
The darker hue is a never-ending plight,
As the darker the berry the sweeter the juice never tasted right
Say my name!! say my name!!
Not blackie, charcoal or midnight
Sarah is my name,
chest out proud standing tall and upright
Ms. Sarah Jones! I belted out bold, forthright,
Not to be mistaken for Midnight

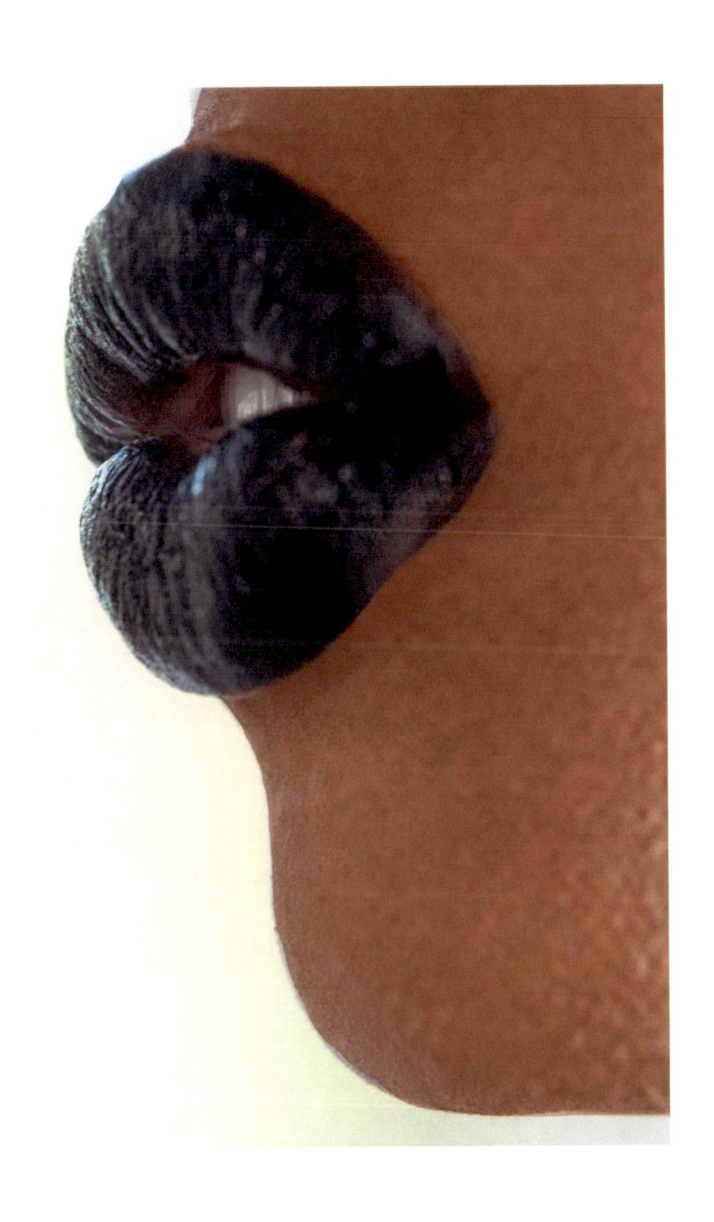

"If I lick your big juicy charcoal lips.
Would it taste like chocolate chips?"

75 | *The Calming Presence*

## Standing Still

When I walk away
It is not because I don't care
The lessons of life have taught me
To plant my feet on solid ground
For the unteachable moments become teachable
When there is little movement
And I stand still

77 | *The Calming Presence*